EMMANUEL JOSEPH

The Algorithmic Appetite, How Robotics and Sociology Influence Culinary Culture

Copyright © 2025 by Emmanuel Joseph

All rights reserved. No part of this publication may be reproduced, stored or transmitted in any form or by any means, electronic, mechanical, photocopying, recording, scanning, or otherwise without written permission from the publisher. It is illegal to copy this book, post it to a website, or distribute it by any other means without permission.

First edition

*This book was professionally typeset on Reedsy.
Find out more at reedsy.com*

Contents

1	Chapter 1: The Dawn of Technological Gastronomy	1
2	Chapter 2: Robots in the Kitchen: Beyond the Cutting Edge	3
3	Chapter 3: The Sociology of Eating: A New Perspective	5
4	Chapter 4: The Algorithmic Chef: Blending Art and Science	7
5	Chapter 5: Culinary Robots in the Global Kitchen	9
6	Chapter 6: The Future of Dining: Experiential Gastronomy	11
7	Chapter 7: The Role of AI in Sustainable Cooking	13
8	Chapter 8: The Ethical Implications of Robotic Cooking	15
9	Chapter 9: The Role of Education in Technological Gastronomy	17
10	Chapter 10: The Impact of Technological Gastronomy on Food...	19
11	Chapter 11: The Role of Cultural Preservation in...	21
12	Chapter 12: The Future of Technological Gastronomy	23
13	Chapter 13: The Rise of Digital Food Communities	25
14	Chapter 14: The Evolution of Food Delivery Services	27
15	Chapter 15: The Impact of Technological Gastronomy on Food...	29
16	Chapter 16: The Intersection of Technology and Nutrition	31
17	Chapter 17: The Role of Culinary Robots in Space Exploration	33
18	Chapter 18: Conclusion: Embracing the Algorithmic Appetite	35

1

Chapter 1: The Dawn of Technological Gastronomy

In the heart of bustling cities and quaint villages alike, the culinary arts have always reflected the heartbeat of society. From grand feasts to humble home-cooked meals, food is a universal language that transcends borders. With the advent of robotics and advanced algorithms, this timeless practice has found new expression, giving rise to what can be called Technological Gastronomy. It is not just about automating kitchens; it's a revolution that blends human creativity with machine precision, pushing the boundaries of what's possible in the culinary world.

This chapter explores the historical context leading to this fusion. From the first mechanical kitchen appliances to the sophisticated robots used in modern restaurants, the journey is both fascinating and pivotal. The pioneers of this movement saw beyond the mere convenience of machines; they envisioned a world where robotics could elevate the art of cooking, making it more precise, efficient, and accessible. This vision laid the foundation for today's advanced culinary technologies.

As we delve deeper, we see how these advancements are not just about convenience but about creating new experiences. Automated kitchens can prepare meals with a level of consistency and precision that humans alone might find challenging. This has led to a new wave of dining experiences, where technology and tradition coexist harmoniously. It's a dance of innovation and heritage, where every dish tells a story of human ingenuity and the relentless march of progress.

Finally, we examine the societal impact of this shift. How has it changed the way we view food, cooking, and dining? Have these innovations made culinary arts more inclusive, allowing more people to experiment and express themselves through food? This chapter sets the stage for an in-depth exploration of how robotics and sociology intertwine in the realm of gastronomy, shaping our culinary culture in unprecedented ways.

2

Chapter 2: Robots in the Kitchen: Beyond the Cutting Edge

Robots in the kitchen are no longer the stuff of science fiction; they are a reality. From chopping vegetables to plating dishes, these mechanical marvels are transforming how we cook and eat. But beyond the obvious benefits of speed and efficiency, what deeper changes are they bringing to our culinary practices? This chapter delves into the technologies behind these innovations and the myriad ways they are reshaping our kitchens.

The emergence of robots capable of performing complex culinary tasks is a testament to advancements in artificial intelligence and machine learning. These machines can learn from thousands of recipes, adjusting cooking techniques and flavor profiles to suit individual preferences. It's not just about replicating human chefs but about enhancing their capabilities. Robots can perform repetitive tasks with unwavering precision, allowing human chefs to focus on creativity and presentation.

However, the integration of robotics into cooking raises important questions. How do these machines affect the authenticity and soul of cooking? Can a robot, despite its precision, replicate the love and care that goes into a home-cooked meal? This chapter explores these philosophical and emotional dimensions, considering how technology can complement rather than replace the human touch in the kitchen.

As we explore the implications of robotic cooking, we also look at its accessibility. These technologies are becoming more affordable, making it possible for home kitchens to benefit from automation. This democratization of technology has the potential to revolutionize home cooking, making it easier for people to prepare healthy, delicious meals with minimal effort. The chapter concludes with a look at future trends, imagining a world where every kitchen has its own robotic assistant, seamlessly blending tradition with innovation.

3

Chapter 3: The Sociology of Eating: A New Perspective

Eating is inherently a social act, deeply rooted in cultural and societal norms. With the rise of technological gastronomy, these norms are evolving. This chapter examines how the integration of robotics into the culinary world is influencing our social behaviors and perceptions around food. It's not just about how we cook but also about how we share meals, experience dining, and connect with one another.

Food has always been a medium for social bonding, from family dinners to community feasts. The introduction of robotic chefs and automated kitchens brings a new dimension to these gatherings. On one hand, it offers unprecedented convenience, allowing people to host elaborate meals with minimal effort. On the other hand, it raises questions about the authenticity and emotional connection involved in preparing and sharing food. Can a meal prepared by a robot carry the same warmth as one made by hand?

This chapter also explores the impact of technological gastronomy on dining experiences outside the home. Restaurants are increasingly adopting robots to enhance service and efficiency. While this can lead to more consistent dining experiences, it also changes the dynamics of hospitality. The personal touch of a chef or server is something many diners cherish. As we embrace these technologies, we must find a balance between efficiency and the human elements that make dining special.

Sociologists are particularly interested in how these changes affect different demographics. Are certain groups more inclined to embrace robotic cooking, while others resist it? How do socioeconomic factors influence access to these technologies? By examining these questions, we gain a deeper understanding of the societal shifts occurring in response to technological advancements in the culinary world.

4

Chapter 4: The Algorithmic Chef: Blending Art and Science

In the age of technological gastronomy, algorithms play a pivotal role in shaping our culinary experiences. These sophisticated programs analyze vast amounts of data to create recipes that cater to individual tastes, dietary needs, and even cultural preferences. This chapter explores the fascinating world of algorithmic cooking, where art and science converge to create unique culinary masterpieces.

At the heart of this revolution is the ability of algorithms to process and learn from a plethora of recipes and cooking techniques. By analyzing patterns and trends, these programs can generate new recipes that push the boundaries of traditional cooking. It's not just about following instructions but about understanding the principles behind them. This allows algorithms to innovate, creating dishes that surprise and delight.

The use of algorithms in cooking also opens up new possibilities for personalization. Imagine a meal plan tailored specifically to your nutritional needs, preferences, and even mood. Algorithms can analyze your eating habits and suggest meals that are not only delicious but also aligned with your health goals. This level of customization was unimaginable just a few years ago, but it is now becoming a reality.

However, the reliance on algorithms raises important questions about creativity and originality. Can a machine-generated recipe truly be considered a work of art? How do we balance the precision of algorithms with the spontaneity and intuition of human cooking? This chapter delves into these debates, highlighting the potential and limitations of algorithmic chefs. It concludes by envisioning a future where human chefs and algorithms collaborate, blending art and science to create culinary wonders.

5

Chapter 5: Culinary Robots in the Global Kitchen

The influence of robotics and algorithms on culinary culture is not confined to any one region. This chapter takes a global perspective, exploring how different cultures are integrating these technologies into their culinary practices. From high-tech sushi chefs in Japan to robotic pizza makers in Italy, the impact of technological gastronomy is felt worldwide.

Each culture brings its unique perspective and traditions to the table, influencing how they adopt and adapt to these technologies. In some regions, robots are embraced for their efficiency and precision, while in others, there is a stronger emphasis on preserving traditional methods. This chapter examines these diverse approaches, highlighting the interplay between innovation and heritage.

One of the most exciting aspects of this global integration is the potential for cross-cultural culinary exchanges. Robots and algorithms can facilitate the blending of different cuisines, creating fusion dishes that celebrate the best of multiple traditions. This not only expands our culinary horizons but also fosters a greater appreciation for the diversity of food cultures around the world.

As we explore these global trends, we also consider the challenges and opportunities they present. How do we ensure that technological advancements benefit all communities, rather than exacerbating existing inequalities? What role do governments and organizations play in promoting equitable access to these technologies? By addressing these questions, we can better understand the global impact of robotics and algorithms on culinary culture.

6

Chapter 6: The Future of Dining: Experiential Gastronomy

The integration of robotics and algorithms into the culinary world is paving the way for new and immersive dining experiences. This chapter explores the concept of experiential gastronomy, where technology and creativity combine to create unique and memorable meals. From interactive dining tables to virtual reality culinary journeys, the future of dining is full of exciting possibilities.

One of the most intriguing developments in this field is the use of multisensory experiences to enhance the enjoyment of food. Imagine dining in a restaurant where the ambiance, lighting, and even the aromas are carefully curated to complement each dish. Robotics and algorithms can create these immersive environments, transporting diners to different worlds with every bite. This chapter delves into the science behind these experiences and the impact they have on our perception of food.

Another key aspect of experiential gastronomy is the role of interactivity. Diners are no longer passive recipients of a meal; they are active participants in the culinary process. From customizing their dishes through interactive menus to engaging with robotic chefs, the dining experience becomes a collaborative and dynamic journey. This chapter explores how these interactions enhance our connection to food and the people who prepare it.

As we look to the future, we also consider the ethical implications of these advancements. How do we balance the desire for innovation with the need to preserve the integrity of culinary traditions? What are the environmental and social impacts of these technologies? By addressing these questions, we can ensure that the future of dining remains both exciting and responsible.

7

Chapter 7: The Role of AI in Sustainable Cooking

Sustainability is a pressing concern in today's world, and the culinary industry is no exception. This chapter explores how artificial intelligence (AI) and robotics can contribute to more sustainable cooking practices. From reducing food waste to optimizing energy use, technology has the potential to make our kitchens more environmentally friendly.

One of the most significant ways AI can promote sustainability is through smart inventory management. Algorithms can analyze consumption patterns and predict future needs, helping restaurants and households reduce waste. By ensuring that ingredients are used efficiently and creatively, AI can minimize the environmental impact of food production and consumption.

Robotics also play a crucial role in sustainability efforts. Automated cooking systems can optimize energy use by adjusting cooking times and temperatures precisely. They can also ensure that ingredients are used efficiently, minimizing waste. For example, robotic chefs can utilize every part of an ingredient, reducing the amount of food that ends up in the trash. This efficiency not only benefits the environment but also leads to cost savings for consumers and businesses alike.

AI and robotics can also support sustainable sourcing practices. By analyzing data on food production and supply chains, these technologies can help identify sustainable and ethical sources of ingredients. This allows consumers to make informed choices about the food they eat, promoting more responsible consumption. Additionally, AI can facilitate the development of new plant-based or lab-grown ingredients, offering sustainable alternatives to traditional animal products.

However, the adoption of these technologies also comes with challenges. There are concerns about the environmental impact of producing and disposing of robotics and AI systems. It's essential to consider the full lifecycle of these technologies, from manufacturing to end-of-life disposal. This chapter addresses these concerns and explores potential solutions, such as designing more sustainable robots and developing recycling programs for electronic waste.

The chapter concludes by envisioning a future where AI and robotics play a central role in promoting sustainable cooking practices. By embracing these technologies, we can create a culinary culture that prioritizes the health of our planet and its inhabitants. It's an exciting and hopeful vision, one that underscores the potential of technology to drive positive change in the world of food.

8

Chapter 8: The Ethical Implications of Robotic Cooking

The integration of robotics and AI into the culinary world raises important ethical questions. This chapter delves into these issues, exploring the moral and societal implications of technological gastronomy. From labor displacement to data privacy, the ethical landscape of robotic cooking is complex and multifaceted.

One of the most pressing concerns is the impact on employment. As robots take over tasks traditionally performed by human workers, there is a risk of job displacement. While automation can lead to increased efficiency and cost savings, it also raises questions about the future of work in the culinary industry. This chapter examines these challenges and discusses potential solutions, such as retraining programs and new job opportunities in the tech-driven culinary landscape.

Another significant ethical consideration is data privacy. AI systems used in cooking often rely on vast amounts of data, including personal preferences and dietary habits. Ensuring that this data is collected and used responsibly is crucial. This chapter explores the measures needed to protect consumer privacy and maintain trust in these technologies.

The chapter also addresses the ethical implications of algorithmic decision-making in cooking. How do we ensure that AI systems make fair and unbiased decisions? What happens when an algorithm makes a mistake in a high-stakes culinary situation? These questions highlight the need for transparency and accountability in the development and deployment of AI in the culinary world.

Finally, this chapter explores the broader societal implications of technological gastronomy. How do these advancements affect our relationship with food and cooking? What values do we prioritize as we integrate technology into our kitchens? By examining these questions, we gain a deeper understanding of the ethical dimensions of robotic cooking and the need for thoughtful and responsible innovation.

9

Chapter 9: The Role of Education in Technological Gastronomy

As robotics and AI become more prevalent in the culinary world, education plays a crucial role in preparing the next generation of chefs and food enthusiasts. This chapter explores the educational initiatives and programs designed to equip individuals with the skills and knowledge needed to navigate this tech-driven culinary landscape.

One of the key aspects of this educational shift is the integration of technology into culinary schools and training programs. Future chefs must learn not only traditional cooking techniques but also how to work with and alongside advanced technologies. This includes understanding the principles of AI and robotics, as well as practical skills in programming and operating automated kitchen systems.

Educational institutions are also increasingly focusing on interdisciplinary approaches, blending culinary arts with fields like computer science and engineering. This cross-disciplinary training equips students with a holistic understanding of technological gastronomy, fostering innovation and creativity. This chapter highlights some of the leading programs and initiatives in this space, showcasing how they are shaping the future of culinary education.

The chapter also explores the importance of lifelong learning in the context of technological gastronomy. As technology continues to evolve, chefs and food professionals must stay updated with the latest advancements. This requires a commitment to continuous education and professional development. From online courses to industry workshops, there are numerous opportunities for individuals to enhance their skills and stay ahead of the curve.

Finally, this chapter examines the role of public education in promoting technological literacy in the culinary world. By raising awareness and understanding of AI and robotics, we can foster a more informed and engaged society. This includes educating consumers about the benefits and challenges of these technologies, empowering them to make informed choices about the food they eat and the technologies they embrace.

10

Chapter 10: The Impact of Technological Gastronomy on Food Security

Technological gastronomy has the potential to address some of the most pressing challenges related to food security. This chapter explores how AI and robotics can contribute to a more resilient and equitable food system, ensuring that everyone has access to safe and nutritious food.

One of the key ways technology can enhance food security is through precision agriculture. AI-driven systems can analyze data on soil conditions, weather patterns, and crop health, enabling farmers to optimize their practices and increase yields. This leads to more efficient use of resources and reduces the risk of crop failures. By enhancing agricultural productivity, AI and robotics can help ensure a stable and reliable food supply.

Robotics also play a crucial role in improving food distribution and reducing waste. Automated systems can streamline the logistics of transporting and storing food, minimizing spoilage and ensuring that food reaches those in need. This is particularly important in regions with limited infrastructure or challenging environmental conditions.

The chapter also examines the role of AI in addressing malnutrition and dietary health. By analyzing data on population health and dietary habits, AI systems can identify nutritional gaps and develop targeted interventions.

This includes personalized meal plans and recommendations that cater to individual needs and preferences, promoting better health outcomes.

However, the implementation of these technologies must be done thoughtfully and inclusively. There are concerns about the digital divide and the accessibility of advanced technologies in low-income and rural areas. This chapter addresses these challenges and explores strategies for ensuring that the benefits of technological gastronomy are shared equitably. By fostering collaboration between governments, organizations, and communities, we can build a more inclusive and resilient food system.

11

Chapter 11: The Role of Cultural Preservation in Technological Gastronomy

While technological gastronomy offers exciting possibilities, it is essential to preserve the rich cultural heritage associated with food and cooking. This chapter explores the balance between innovation and tradition, highlighting the importance of cultural preservation in the age of robotics and AI.

Food is deeply intertwined with cultural identity, and traditional cooking techniques are often passed down through generations. As we embrace technological advancements, there is a risk of losing these cherished traditions. This chapter examines how we can integrate technology into the culinary world without compromising cultural heritage.

One approach is to use technology to document and preserve traditional recipes and cooking methods. AI can analyze and catalog these practices, ensuring that they are not lost to time. Additionally, robots can be programmed to replicate traditional techniques with precision, allowing for the faithful reproduction of cultural dishes.

The chapter also explores the role of culinary tourism in cultural preservation. Technology can enhance the tourism experience by offering immersive and interactive culinary journeys. From virtual reality tours of traditional kitchens to AI-guided cooking classes, these experiences can promote cultural appreciation and preservation.

Moreover, this chapter highlights the importance of community involvement in technological gastronomy. By engaging with local communities and respecting their culinary traditions, we can create a collaborative and inclusive approach to innovation. This includes supporting initiatives that empower traditional cooks and artisans, ensuring that their knowledge and skills are valued and preserved.

Finally, the chapter addresses the broader societal implications of cultural preservation in technological gastronomy. How do we balance the desire for innovation with the need to honor and protect our culinary heritage? What role do policymakers and organizations play in promoting cultural preservation? By addressing these questions, we can ensure that technological advancements enrich, rather than erode, our cultural identity.

12

Chapter 12: The Future of Technological Gastronomy

As we conclude our exploration of technological gastronomy, this chapter looks to the future. What can we expect in the coming years as AI and robotics continue to advance? How will these technologies shape the culinary landscape and our relationship with food?

One of the most exciting possibilities is the continued evolution of personalized dining experiences. AI-driven systems will become even more sophisticated, offering unprecedented levels of customization. Imagine a world where your meals are tailored to your exact preferences and nutritional needs, with robots preparing dishes that are as unique as you are.

Another key trend is the integration of AI and robotics into every aspect of the food supply chain. From farm to table, these technologies will optimize efficiency, reduce waste, and enhance sustainability. This holistic approach will create a more resilient and equitable food system, capable of meeting the challenges of a growing global population.

The chapter also explores the potential for new culinary innovations. As AI and robotics become more advanced, we can expect to see the development of entirely new cooking techniques and flavor profiles. This will push the boundaries of what we consider possible in the culinary world, opening up exciting opportunities for chefs and food enthusiasts.

Finally, this chapter envisions a future where technological gastronomy fosters greater cultural exchange and understanding. By embracing the diversity of food cultures around the world, we can create a global culinary community that celebrates both innovation and tradition. This vision underscores the potential of technology to bring us closer together, transcending borders and building a more connected and harmonious world.

In conclusion, "The Algorithmic Appetite: How Robotics and Sociology Influence Culinary Culture" explores the fascinating intersection of technology and culinary arts. From the dawn of technological gastronomy to the future of dining, this book offers a comprehensive and thought-provoking look at how robotics and AI are reshaping our culinary culture. As we navigate this exciting journey, we must balance innovation with tradition, ensuring that technological advancements enrich our culinary experiences while preserving the cultural heritage that makes food so special.

13

Chapter 13: The Rise of Digital Food Communities

In the digital age, online communities have become a significant aspect of how we interact with food. From recipe-sharing forums to social media groups, these virtual spaces allow people to connect, share, and learn about culinary practices from around the world. This chapter explores the role of digital food communities in shaping culinary culture and how they are influenced by technological advancements.

Digital food communities provide a platform for people to share their culinary creations, exchange recipes, and offer cooking tips. These interactions foster a sense of belonging and camaraderie among members, creating a global network of food enthusiasts. The rise of food bloggers and influencers has further amplified the reach of these communities, turning them into powerful drivers of culinary trends.

Technology plays a crucial role in facilitating these connections. AI-powered platforms can recommend recipes based on user preferences, create virtual cooking classes, and even connect users with chefs for personalized advice. These innovations enhance the sense of community and make it easier for people to engage with food in meaningful ways.

However, the digitalization of food communities also raises challenges. Issues such as misinformation, cultural appropriation, and the commercialization of culinary content can impact the authenticity and integrity of these spaces. This chapter examines these challenges and discusses ways to foster inclusive and respectful digital food communities.

14

Chapter 14: The Evolution of Food Delivery Services

Food delivery services have undergone a significant transformation with the advent of technology. From traditional takeout to app-based delivery platforms, the way we order and receive food has changed dramatically. This chapter explores the evolution of food delivery services and the impact of robotics and AI on this industry.

The introduction of AI and robotics has revolutionized food delivery logistics. Algorithms can optimize delivery routes, predict demand, and ensure timely deliveries. Some companies are even experimenting with autonomous delivery vehicles and drones, promising faster and more efficient service. These innovations have the potential to reshape the food delivery landscape, offering unprecedented convenience to consumers.

The chapter also examines the impact of these technologies on the restaurant industry. Food delivery platforms have opened up new revenue streams for restaurants, allowing them to reach a broader customer base. However, there are concerns about the impact on traditional dining experiences and the financial pressures on small businesses. This chapter explores these dynamics and discusses strategies for balancing innovation with the sustainability of the restaurant industry.

As we look to the future, the integration of AI and robotics into food delivery services continues to evolve. From personalized meal recommendations to contactless delivery options, technology is enhancing the convenience and safety of food delivery. This chapter concludes by envisioning the future of food delivery and its implications for consumers and businesses alike.

15

Chapter 15: The Impact of Technological Gastronomy on Food Media

Food media has always played a significant role in shaping our culinary culture, from cookbooks and television shows to food blogs and social media. With the rise of technological gastronomy, food media is undergoing a transformation. This chapter explores how AI and robotics are influencing food media and the way we consume culinary content.

AI-powered tools are changing the way food content is created and shared. Algorithms can analyze trends, predict audience preferences, and even generate content. This allows for more targeted and personalized culinary content, catering to the diverse interests of food enthusiasts. For example, AI can generate recipe videos based on popular searches or create virtual cooking tutorials that adapt to the viewer's skill level.

Robotics also play a role in food media. Automated cameras and drones can capture stunning visuals of food preparation and presentation, offering new perspectives and enhancing the viewer experience. These technologies enable content creators to produce high-quality and engaging food media, captivating audiences with visually appealing and informative content.

However, the rise of technological gastronomy in food media also raises questions about authenticity and creativity. Can AI-generated content truly capture the passion and artistry of human chefs? How do we ensure that the cultural and personal stories behind food are not lost in the pursuit of technological innovation? This chapter delves into these debates and highlights the importance of balancing technology with the human touch in food media.

16

Chapter 16: The Intersection of Technology and Nutrition

As technology continues to advance, its impact on nutrition and dietary habits becomes increasingly significant. This chapter explores how AI and robotics are transforming the field of nutrition, offering new tools and insights for promoting healthier eating habits and addressing dietary challenges.

AI-powered nutrition apps can analyze individual dietary habits, provide personalized meal plans, and offer real-time feedback on food choices. These tools empower consumers to make informed decisions about their diet, helping them achieve their health goals. For example, AI can recommend nutrient-rich recipes based on dietary preferences, allergies, and nutritional needs, making it easier for people to eat healthily.

Robotics also contribute to the field of nutrition by assisting in food preparation and portion control. Automated systems can precisely measure ingredients, ensuring that meals are nutritionally balanced and tailored to individual needs. This is particularly beneficial for people with specific dietary requirements, such as those managing chronic conditions or following specialized diets.

The chapter also examines the role of technology in addressing global nutrition challenges. AI can analyze large-scale data on food production, distribution, and consumption, identifying patterns and potential interventions. This information can inform policies and programs aimed at improving nutrition and reducing food insecurity.

As we explore these advancements, it's important to consider the ethical implications. How do we ensure that AI and robotics are used responsibly in the field of nutrition? What measures are needed to protect consumer privacy and prevent the misuse of nutritional data? By addressing these questions, we can harness the potential of technology to promote healthier and more sustainable dietary practices.

17

Chapter 17: The Role of Culinary Robots in Space Exploration

As humanity sets its sights on space exploration, the role of culinary robots becomes increasingly relevant. This chapter explores how AI and robotics are being used to address the unique challenges of cooking and dining in space, offering insights into the future of culinary culture beyond Earth.

Space missions require careful planning and resource management, and food is a critical component. Traditional cooking methods are often impractical in a microgravity environment, necessitating innovative solutions. Culinary robots and AI-powered systems can prepare meals with precision and efficiency, ensuring that astronauts have access to nutritious and palatable food.

AI plays a crucial role in designing space-friendly recipes and meal plans. By analyzing the nutritional needs of astronauts and the constraints of space travel, AI can develop menus that optimize health and performance. These systems can also adapt to individual preferences, providing a sense of comfort and familiarity in the challenging environment of space.

Robotics are also essential for food preparation and storage in space. Automated systems can handle tasks such as rehydrating meals, mixing ingredients, and even growing fresh produce in controlled environments.

These technologies help maintain food quality and safety, contributing to the overall well-being of astronauts.

The chapter also considers the broader implications of culinary technology in space exploration. As we envision long-term missions to Mars and beyond, the ability to prepare and enjoy food will play a vital role in sustaining human life and morale. Culinary robots and AI systems will be at the forefront of these efforts, pushing the boundaries of what is possible in the realm of space gastronomy.

18

Chapter 18: Conclusion: Embracing the Algorithmic Appetite

As we conclude our exploration of technological gastronomy, it's clear that robotics and sociology are profoundly shaping our culinary culture. From the precision of robotic chefs to the personalized recipes generated by AI algorithms, the fusion of technology and food is opening up new possibilities and challenges.

This book has journeyed through the history and evolution of technological gastronomy, examined the societal implications, and envisioned the future of dining. It has highlighted the importance of balancing innovation with cultural preservation, and the need for ethical considerations in the adoption of these technologies. The world of food is evolving, and as we embrace these changes, we must remain mindful of the values and traditions that have always made culinary culture so rich and diverse.

The Algorithmic Appetite invites us to look at food through a new lens, one where technology and human creativity coexist and complement each other. As we move forward, let's celebrate the possibilities that technological gastronomy offers while cherishing the timeless traditions that connect us to our past and to each other.

Thank you for joining me on this culinary adventure. May your future meals be as innovative and delightful as the journey we've taken together in these pages.

Description: Embracing the Algorithmic Appetite

As we reach the end of our exploration into the world of technological gastronomy, it's clear that robotics and sociology are profoundly shaping our culinary culture. From the precision of robotic chefs to the personalized recipes generated by AI algorithms, the fusion of technology and food is opening up new possibilities and challenges.

This book has journeyed through the history and evolution of technological gastronomy, examined the societal implications, and envisioned the future of dining. It has highlighted the importance of balancing innovation with cultural preservation, and the need for ethical considerations in the adoption of these technologies. The world of food is evolving, and as we embrace these changes, we must remain mindful of the values and traditions that have always made culinary culture so rich and diverse.

The Algorithmic Appetite invites us to look at food through a new lens, one where technology and human creativity coexist and complement each other. As we move forward, let's celebrate the possibilities that technological gastronomy offers while cherishing the timeless traditions that connect us to our past and to each other.

Thank you for joining me on this culinary adventure. May your future meals be as innovative and delightful as the journey we've taken together in these pages.

www.ingramcontent.com/pod-product-compliance
Lightning Source LLC
LaVergne TN
LVHW010441070526
838199LV00066B/6118